The Trackway of the Cross

by Alan Shore

with contributions from
Leonard Sanders and John Roberts;
edited with further notes by Hilary Rimmer
and sketches by Liz Johnson.

The speculative history of a pathway
trodden by 6th century monks
from the Lleyn Peninsular to Bangor-is-y-coed
on the River Dee.

*QuercuS

D1208583

****

Quercus
John Roberts
8 Hillside Close, Bartley Green
Birmingham B32 4LT
****

The Trackway of the Cross

by Alan Shore

ISBN 1 898136 02 5

First Published 1993

*
QuercuS

... publishing interesting books ...

Quercus is a regional publisher specialising in books about Wales
and the western Midlands (meaning the West Midlands, Warwickshire,
Worcestershire, Shropshire and south Staffs).

We are interested in the region yesterday, today and tomorrow; in
landscapes and language, trees meadows and flowers, history,
battles, lords and kings, castles and churches, bridges and tunnels.
We want to know about industries and towns, people and customs, parks
and playgrounds, myths and hauntings. In fact we are interested in
any subject that we think you will find interesting.

"The Trackway of the Cross" is the first Quercus title and will soon
be followed by "Australian Williams". William Williams of Pentraeth,
Sir Fon worked his passage to Australia, dug for gold, found it, and
came home to found a building firm in Liverpool. He taught himself to
read and write in English and Welsh and the story is based on his
diaries.

Future titles include "Midland Woods & Forests" "Midland Rivers &
Streams", "Midland Lakes & Ponds", "Midlands Parks" "Midland Castles"
and "Haunted Buildings in the Midlands". "Sketches of Halesowen" is
almost ready, perhaps to be followed by collections of pen and ink
drawings of other places.

We are always willing to discuss ideas and proposals for new titles.
If you have an idea but do not think you are up to writing about it,
talk to us anyway. John Roberts might suggest coauthorship with you
providing the research.

8 Hillside Close, Bartley Green, Birmingham
B32 4LT   021 550 3158

WALKWAYS

DaywalkS Footpath Networks

Arden
Cannock Chase
Chaddesley Woods
Clent & Lickey Hills
Elan Valley
Vale of Llangollen
Wyre Forest

The first four are currently in folded A2
sheet format, sold in a plastic cover.

*

Strolls & Walks

From each of about twenty places there is a
stroll of a mile of so and a walk of 4 or 5 miles.

Strolls & Walks from Picnic Places (Midlands)
Strolls & Walks from Cotswold Villages
Strolls & Walks from Midland Villages

Long Distance Routes

Step by step guides in both directions which
often connect with each other and Long Distance
Footpaths. (A2 sheets folded to A5,
but Heart of England Way is a book.)

Llangollen to Bala   Bala to Snowdon
Birmingham to Ludlow   Ludlow to Rhayader
Rhayader to Aberystwyth
Birmingham to Church Stretton
Heart of England Way

8 Hillside Close, Bartley Green, Birmingham B32 4LT
(Send sae for current list & prices.)

Preface

Alan Shore was born in Smethwick in 1902 and became a foundry engineer with W & T Avery, the Birmingham scale makers. He and his father George were the last survivors of an old Cheshire family, and were associated with the firm for over 100 years. Alan became General Superintendent of all the Avery foundries which were in Leeds, Birmingham and Tame Bridge until he retired in 1967. He was at one time President of the Midland Branch of the Institute of British Foundrymen and the last manager of the famous Soho Foundry, founded by Matthew Boulton and James Watt.

Alan Shore was an interesting man to meet because he had many interests. Although he earned his living in the practical business of casting iron, his romantic quest was the Trackway which he pursued from 1944 until the 1980's. Alan the wood carver turned out splendid little figures, and the bookbinder put The Book of Kells and other classics between handsome tooled leather covers. He was the sort of person that you were always pleased to meet or to hear from.

Alan wrote to John Roberts in 1985 about a Long Distance Footpath that John had written and published under his WALKWAYS imprint. The route ran from Llangollen to Snowdon and Alan wanted to see if any of it coincided with his Trackway. Some parts did so they corresponded and met. Out of interest and pleasure in the landscape, John carried out some fieldwork and footwork to supplement Alan's research, extended the manuscript and produced a photocopied version.

By this time, in 1988, Alan was far from well. Sadly and painfully he declined as the months went by. After his death in 1989 the papers lay unused, and it was not until 1991 that John Roberts started his Quercus imprint and his thoughts turned to the possibility of publishing The Trackway of the Cross. He approached me as a lecturer in Geography for some professional input in the editing of the book. I have also a long standing interest in the ancient past of the Lleyn Peninsular at the western end of the Trackway. We are very grateful to Alan's widow Marion for agreeing to let us publish Alan's work.

The book is in no way a conventional history. It is about the past, but the usual historical sources of evidence are largely missing; 6th century monks did not leave maps or manuscripts of travellers tales. Written sources show beyond doubt that the places at both ends of the Trackway existed at the relevant time. Then there is the physical and historical evidence of intermediate places which these travellers are likely to have visited. Some conclusions are forced on us by the geography of North Wales, which compelled travellers to take certain directions. But the actual existence of the Trackway is a deduction and a hypothesis rather than a fact, and readers can attached what degree of probability they wish.

For these reasons we have subtitled the book "a speculative history", and because it suggests why pursuit of the idea so absorbed Alan Shore. Historical or other facts are all very well, but what drives researchers and archaeologists, historians and scientists, journalists and detectives, economists and political commentators, and what makes life interesting for us all, is to speculate on what might be, and to try and find out. So the Trackway is also the story of Alan Shore's speculative quest into the sixth century.

Readers of this book can accept the Trackway as an absorbing idea, and they can read more about its times. But they can also use the detailed description to follow the Trackway on the ground. Most of it is within reach of some sort of road or lane and significant sections can be walked, as they are public rights of way. You will meet a spectrum of scenic contrasts; jagged mountain ridges, deep narrow valleys, moody and glittering lakes, rolling grassland, moors and marshes, and the clay and boulder cliffs facing the sea.

What follows is largely the original work of Alan Shore with additions (which Alan notes) by John Roberts and Leonard Sanders. I have been able to contribute some extra notes and to advise a few minor rearrangements of paragraphs.

Finally, although the book is about Wales and Welsh history, it was written in English by an Englishman. To translate odd passages or otherwise garnish it with Welsh would have been to dress it in artificial costume. Sufficient that Alan knew that Wales is not just a western part of England and was respectful of the names and traditions.

Hilary Rimmer

Marion and Alan Shore in 1987

Contents

Introduction

"The fact of the matter is that the subject of a lecture is apt to
prove too rich for summary treatment. When certain kinds of books
come in, it is difficult to keep them out. And as soon as the first
step is taken in venturing a little further afield, a bounteous, an
illimitable prospect beckons the explorer on, even though, as in this
case, he may have nothing but the candle of curiosity and the will 'o
the wisp of enquiring ignorance to light him on his way. He may not
even have set out in the right direction."

From the Introduction to "Desert Islands"
by Walter de la Mare, 1930.

* * * * *

"The Trackway of the Cross" is the name I gave to what seemed to me
to be a route running east across the mountains of North Wales. I was
first attracted by the words, on Bartholomew's half inch map "Ancient
Trackway". This was at a weekend break during the last war, when en
route for Snowdon I walked over to Llyn Gwynant from Dolwyddelan.

Since then over the years, investigating the feasibility of a
continuous track of about 60 miles from the coast to the River Dee
has given me many happy hours of employment. The following account
is an attempt to record the progress of the investigation as my ideas
changed with increasing knowledge.

Originally these ideas were based on the assumption that the
following three statements were correct: A pathway marked "Ancient
Trackway" on Bartholomew's Map was indeed ancient; "Croes", a name
which occurs several times on the route is Welsh for cross, and means
that it is a religious symbol; the track is on a ley or is determined
by a series of leys.

As the investigation continued, I began to realise that all three
suppositions could and probably would prove unsound. For instance,
"croes" may just refer to intersecting routes.

Yet in spite of these undoubted shaky foundations, what I think is
intriguing is that they seem to have lead to a correct conclusion.
Eminent authorities, who have so kindly considered my ideas, have
been ready to accept the possibility, or even probability, of the
existence of such a route. I have refered to some of their comments

here, and a letter from Professor RJC Atkinson appears with his kind permission as an Appendix. They point out, however, the impossibility of fixing with certainty a route used 1200 or more years ago.

I am convinced that "The Trackway" was the way the Saints took going east from the coast and later by the Pilgrims journeying west to Bardsey.

What is most important, it directed me to Bangor is y Coed, that great early seventh century "monastery under the wood" with much fascinating material to "unearth", though no evidence of its existence on site.

Having failed to find anyone who has written before me on this particular subject I have thought it worthwhile setting down my findings in the following records. It first took the form of a paper delivered to a local society in Morfa Nefin in September 1972. There have been various additions and modifications in the light of further investigations, particularly the exploration of the eastern section (Bryn Eglwys to Bangor) by Leonard Sanders in 1982, and of the entire route by John Roberts in 1987.

Mr Watkins and Straight Tracks

My father, who was born before the advent of the motor car, was a dedicated walker. As a Victorian he was happy with a day's jaunt of 30 or 40 miles. When I was sixteen I made my longest walk ever with him. We tramped 45 miles and got home to cocoa and kippers in the early hours of the morning.

He was dedicated to short cuts which mostly proved to be only short on the map; for, contending there was no law of trespass, he frequently had to spend time convincing farmers and gamekeepers who did not see eye to eye with him.

Though we favoured fields and moorlands, it was still possible sixty or seventy years ago, to walk along our roads without fear of sudden death and so sometimes we used them also. We were much impressed with the straightness of the Roman roads which demonstrated so plainly their authors' singleness of purpose.

One day in 1929, when I was rambling with friends along a track over the Surrey hills, I mentioned our practice of following a compass course or making a bee line for some prominent object, when one of the company said: "You ought to meet Uncle Alfred. I must get him to send you his book." She was as good as her word and I soon received "The Ley Hunter's Manual" (see Reading List), inscribed "Good luck to a ley-hunter, Alfred Watkins, June 1929."

After my father and I had read his Manual we bought his other books on the subject and, wherever we went, we were always on the lookout for the Old Straight Track.

As everyone may not be familiar with Watkins' idea of the Old Straight Track, or "Ley" as he liked to call it, I should, I think, now briefly describe it. He suggested that the early inhabitants of these islands moved from place to place along straight lines which were originally sighted on prominent natural features such as hill peaks or notches in the skyline or clumps of trees. He further contended that if you applied a ruler to a map to join two such features (far apart but in sight of one another) you would often find that the line went through man made objects like camps, crosses, old churches, moats and ponds, mark stone and cairns, and often included ancient fords and bits of paved trackway. Further confirmation of the line of a ley could be had from a study of the names of the places it passed through.

Nowadays Watkins is out of favour with serious archaeologists who are inclined to smile at his simplicity. That he claimed too much in his enthusiasm is certain, for he linked up on paper objects which, though spatially near, were in fact widely separated in period of time. Nevertheless, I am sure he was "on the right track" so to speak; for if one wishes to travel on foot between two distant places, through an unmapped terrain devoid of any roads, surely one tries to follow as straight a course as possible. The nature of the ground may make it impossible to move exactly on the line of sight, still one keeps as near to it as one can. (But see notes in "Magic Ley Lines" 1978 to show how opinions can change since this was first written in 1968.)

[Alfred Watkins's deductions are not the sort of stuff to be taken too seriously, but you could claim for him that his enthusiastic speculation endowed landscapes with a new significance for many people. They were encouraged to examine and wonder. Ed]

Ancient Track: First Ideas

During the Second World War in September 1944 I managed to take two days holiday, and walked due west from Dolwyddelan to Llyn Gwynant along what the map described as an "Ancient Trackway".

Some years later I went east, that is in the opposite direction, from Dolwyddelan over the Bwlch y groes to Penmachno on what appeared to be a continuation of this track. I was curious to know how ancient the trackway was and what places it connected up - so, practising Ley technique, I laid a ruler on the map and continued the straight line east and west. On this line, towards the sea 16 miles away to the west was Pen y groes and 29 miles to the east was Valle Crucis Abbey. I had already been over one Bwlch y groes near Penmachno; I found another on the track line over Llantysilio mountain near Valle Crucis. All these references to the CROSS made me think that the route might be a religious one, connecting perhaps Valle Crucis with Ireland. This assumption seemed further to be confirmed when I discovered a hospice, Yspyty Ifan, also on the track. However, as it turned out, this was not the proper conclusion; though I did not know it then, I had fallen into the ley hunter's trap of not checking dates.

[Alan later notes that the hospice was founded in 1120 as a hostel for travellers. The name means "John's Hospice". It may in fact have some connection with his Trackway as he mentions in his closing notes. Ed]

When I retired I decided to research the Trackway more thoroughly by a course of reading coupled with visits to locations. I found, as Watkins had found before me, very little had been written about tracks in general, and I could uncover nothing at all about the trackway in which I was interested until William Condry in "Exploring Wales" 1970 wrote: "The medieval track that went west from this castle (Dolwyddelan) through the moors to Nant Gwynant still exists. So does the pack horse trail that went from Dolwyddelan to Penmachno." By 1970 however I reckoned I knew a deal more than that about this trackway.

The Trackway of the Cross

For identification, I called the route "The Trackway of THE CROSS" because the word appears in Pen y Groes, Bwlch y Groes (twice) and Valle Crucis. "Croes" may not mean anything more than a "crossing" as, for instance, in: croeslon, a crosslane. However, I think it has a religious significance; if this is so, the naming would not be earlier than the fifth century.

The Chi Rho was the original symbol used by the Christians, essentially an X superimposed upon a P and derived from the Greek letters X - chi and P - rho, the initial letters of the words "X Ploros" or "Christos anointed". This symbol was sometimes simplified to a P with horizontal line across, giving a headed version of the later Cross. The Cross as such did not take its place until after the abolition of crucifixion by Constantine AD 288-337. In fact it did not come into general use until the fifth century. (The earliest representation of the true cross in Wales that can be dated is the Cadfan Stone, Anglesey, AD 625.)

I find "crucis" in Valle Crucis does not refer to the abbey but rather it is derived from a stone cross in the valley, the Eliseg memorial pillar c 800. The abbey was not established until 1201.

Considerations, which will appear later, lead me to feel that the Trackway came into prominence in the Age of the Saints, i.e. the first part of the seventh or the later part of the sixth century, when the peregrini were moving inwards across Britain from the Irish coast. Sir J.E. Lloyd in his "History of Wales" says: "The sixth century saint was habitually a migrant, regarding the call of pilgrimage and travel in distant lands as a high spiritual distinction." Migration was most frequently east, probably taking for example the saints' journeyings in the Egyptian desert. Valle Crucis must obviously be ruled out as a fitting destination as it does not belong to that age. However, following the direct line a few more miles eastward the ancient site of Bangor is y coed is reached; it was a place of distinction in the 6th century completely satisfying the requirements for a terminal point.

Both Bangor and Clynnog were in the eighth century "Mother Churches of Wales" but both were established long before. Bangor was in existence prior to the Battle of Chester AD 616 and Clynnog has a "clas" (group of churches) founded by St. Beuno round about this date. St. Beuno crops up again twice along the track - Gwyddelwern is dedicated to him and his holy well is at Betws Gwerfyl Goch.

Alan Shore's hand drawn and coloured map: 1972

(6)

It will be noticed that the Trackway of the Cross runs on, or very close to, the 53rd parallel of latitude throughout almost all of its sixty mile journey; nowhere does it depart from it by more than four miles to the north or one mile to the south. Both terminals are almost dead on - Clynnog deviating about one minute of a degree and Bangor six seconds. No real significance need be attributed to this fact except to show that this Trackway does run truly east west.

However it is remarkable that exactly on the 53rd parallel due west across the sea and ten miles inland from the coast of Ireland is the ancient monastery complex of Glendalough: oratory, cathedral, cross, round tower and churches. Founded by St Kevin in 520, it survived as a monastic city until the seventeenth century. He is reported as dying in 618 three years after the battle of Chester (when the Bangor monks were killed), and the reputed date of the foundation of the Clynnog community. Thus space and time are neatly tied up.

In spite of this coincidence of dates, I believe that the Trackway, or a large section of, it existed long before the sixth century, for a number of "camps" are right on the sight lines. Still, I feel that it came into prominence as west-east route during the Age of Saints and it was the route taken by the original peregrini who peopled Bangor is y coed, travelling from the civilised Celtic region to the barbarous unknown of the Midland forest.

[Alan here refers to the earthwork fortifications which can usually be traced to the Iron Age. It is not clear whether they were simply forts or permanent settlements, it probably depended on the site and the times. Ed]

In his otherwise excellent book on "The Settlements of the Celtic Saints in Wales" Professor E G Bowen makes a sweeping statement. He says; "the only possible parallel for the Llandovery-Brecon-Abergaveny transverse route in the north would be the Bala Cleft route linking the fort *[Roman]* at Caergai with that at Ffrith; but even this cannot be traced with accuracy across the Merionethshire mountains of the west coast."

Certainly the Trackway of the Cross would be a feasible east west route. The Professor seems to hold essentially to the idea that the Roman road system was the only practicable means of long distance travel; but the natives moved around before the Romans arrived and after they left. In Anglo Saxon England the new inhabitants largely ignored the Roman roads and in consequence they fell into decay. In at least one case the site of a Roman road became a burial ground.

[Roads are built or natural ways used according to need; direction is the main factor but the nature of the traffic has a major influence. The Romans needed straight level routes suitable for big groups of travellers and wheeled supply carts. And they had organisation and resources to engineer roads. The Celts and Anglo Saxons (and particularly itinerant monks) travelled on foot or horseback, and where any distance was involved moved goods by packhorse. Steeper, narrower and unsurfaced routes could be and had to be used, since these societies lacked the structure and resources of the Roman Empire. Ed.]

Later, after discussing St Beuno dedications at Gwyddelwern and Betws Gwelfyl Goch and the group in Lleyn, Professor Bowen says; "Exactly how this Venodotian group of churches was linked with the Powysian one is not known, but the use of the former Roman road system is indicated." And again; "there is considerably more map evidence to show that St Beuno in the sixth century was following what remained of the Roman roads to get from Powys to north west Wales than there is to suggest that he followed the prehistoric trackway over the mountains that Sir Cyril Fox has traced so clearly from the bend of the Severn near Shrewsbury on to the Menai Straits." (Routes was: Berwyn range, Dee south of Corwen, Conway, Snowdon area, Menai.) Perhaps Sir Cyril Fox's route was not the one used, surely there were other ancient ways, such as the Trackway of the Cross.

I now believe that the Trackway of the Cross runs some 60 miles, due east, from the shallow Irish facing coast just north of Clynnog fawr, in a practically straight line, through the mountains to Bangor is y coed on the River Dee.

[Alan Shore felt that his Trackway was taken by monks in the Dark Ages, but it is likely that these natural ways were used for many centuries before. The point is made by Professor Atkinson in his letter in the Appendix. Immovable landmarks such as natural clefts or passes between mountains must have been prominent markers for much earlier people. Ed]

The Dark Ages

Before examining the Trackway in detail, it is helpful to look at the Ordnance Survey Dark Ages Sketch Map for the period AD 400 to 800. I have incorporated the relevant details into my general map (pages 22 & 23). This map is of a part of Britain now called North Wales; it shows probable survivals of the Roman occupation, which ceased officially in AD 410. Circles represent Roman forts and their linking roads are indicated. These forts were of no use to the Britons so they soon became ruinous and later too the roads decayed.

It would be too confusing to try to indicate all early Christian shrines but the sites of all known monastic and clas communities are marked. Probably the most important and the largest were founded by St Deiniol, Bangor in Arfon and Bangor on Dee (Bangor is y coed), yet Clynnog Fawr founded by St Beuno was also of renown.

The Anglo Saxon dykes of Wat and Offa are shown for reference, but these were not built until after the period of Celtic religious activity.

Notes to the OS Dark Ages Map make it plain that hardly any fifth to ninth century place names are known with any certainty. We have to rely on archaeological evidence for sites and later recorded oral tradition for names. Facts relating to people are still more vague. The chief sources of information are:

> The Venerable Bede AD 673 - 735 the famous monk of Wearmouth and Jarrow who wrote "A History of the English Church and People"

> Gildas and Nennius - monks who wrote in the sixth century

> The Anglo Saxon Chronicle - contemporary accounts written between AD 530 and 1000

> Annales Cambriae ("Welsh Annals") written AD 600 and 1000

> Brut y Twysogion, Chronicles of the Welsh Princes AD 700 - 1050

Particulars about saints like Illtyd, Gamon, Cybi, Seriol, Teilo, Cadoc, Padarn, Beuno, Deiniol and a host of others, which are related in their "Lives", can only be accepted with considerable reserve. With one or two exceptions, their exploits have about as much existence in fact as those of the heroes of Mabinogion, a group of romantic, not to say highly improbable, stories of Welsh heroes containing many of the early Celtic sources of the Arthurian legend. The saints "Lives" were often manufactured by over zealous fourteenth century monks 700 years or so after the supposed events occurred. They were expert at concocting stories to get money from pilgrims - even bigger liars than modern publicity practitioners and salesmen. Mr. W.H. Davis in a paper contributed in 1967 to a conference on "Christianity in Britain 300 - 700" (see Reading List), says "The saints of history have largely been swamped by the saints of legend." He confirms the reality of the monastic founders like Illtyd, Cadog, David and Deiniol, but one must bear in mind that a church bearing a saint's name is not alone proof that he founded it. It may have been established long after his death by his "cult" or following.

At this point, preparing for my Morfa Nefin talk in 1972, I drew a series of tentative lines on a map which I thought might indicate a possible route between Clynog Fawr and Bangor is y coed. These were rather more subtle than my original crude but revealing straight "ley lines". Connecting churches and crosses and old tracks and bearing in mind the contours of hills and valleys, it seemed to me that my idea was perhaps a little more than tenable.

I realised that a route could not be treated as established, even as a possibility until every mile had been traversed. In 1985 I bought two Long Distance Footpath routes by John Roberts in his Walkways series - Llangollen to Bala and Bala to Snowdon, just from curiosity. But I found that from the head of Llyn Gwynant near Snowdon to Ysbytty Ifan he had followed exactly the route I had in mind. This was not very surprising since it is one of the best known long continuous non road routes in North Wales, which may have something to do with ancient origins.

It was not until 1987 that John Roberts studied the route of "The Trackway of the Cross" and his contribution is included in what follows.

Ways and Means

The sixth century Christians left us no maps or instructions, so this cannot be a detailed and precise account of their route across North Wales. Whilst we can say that they would probably have travelled from one friendly church to another through a hostile landscape, and we think we know their destination, who can say how they went between stops? This is an attempted reconstruction or speculation about the behaviour of certain people 1400 years ago. It is not possible to prove that it is correct, only that a certain path seems more or less probable than another.

Sketch maps are provided to help you follow the route. They show monasteries and churches, rivers and mountains, the Roman roads and a few anachronisms such as modern towns and roads. Anachronisms may not be totally out of place because the existence of a modern road suggests an older, perhaps ancient, track formed where the going was easiest.

You will certainly find this speculation more interesting and enjoyable if you can follow it on Ordnance Survey Maps. The Landranger Series (1:50,000 - 1.25 inches to the mile, or 2 cms to the kilometre) are very adequate, and you would need sheets 115 Snowdon, 116 Denbigh and Colwyn Bay, and 117 Chester.

To work out a route from the clues we have been left is very difficult but in some places they are stronger and more helpful than others. Here and there we can say that the monks must have taken a particular route because there really is no other. Mountains, marshes and rivers determined the route of the monks in the same way that they have determined much of history. This is true, for example of the approach to the Snowdon massif from the coast to Rhyd Ddu.

In other places the route is at first almost surprising. For example, leaving the head of Llyn Gwynant, the route to Dolwyddelan seems far from obvious, and is not too easy to see on the ground. But look again at the massed crags on the Landranger map and see how this way, through Bwlch Ehediad, is the shortest and lowest eastward mountain crossing for many miles to the north or south. And it is confirmed by the existence of the "ancient track" along that way (which first sparked Alan Shore's interest) and an early church at Dolwyddelan. In complete contrast, at the eastern end of the Trackway, there is speculation about three and more possible routes from Bryneglwys to Bangor is y coed and one guess is as good as another.

Adding to the difficulties of inferring a route from clues are changes in the landscape. The high peaks and moors are the part of the British landscape that have changed least over the centuries. But agriculture has cleared woodland and cultivated wild grass moors, and the effects on this route can be seen between Cerigydrudion and Bryneglwys. Mining and quarrying have radically affected some landscapes, for example in the Nantlle Valley. Changes of rainfall patterns, silting of lakes, improved or worsened drainage may have turned swamps into dry land or the reverse. Road, railway and house building have brought changes. And on the west coast where the monks would have landed in Wales from Ireland, there are cliffs of easily eroded boulder clay. Who can say where a coast line of this composition may have lain 1400 years ago?

When trying to assess a route which might have been taken by a particular group of people it seems sensible to try and form some impression of what sort of people they were.

No doubt, in general they were much tougher than most of us. Wet and cold weather were not discomforts that could be avoided, but inevitable features of life. Praying on cold stone floors and wearing coarse woollen robes, they cleared the ground of rocks by hand, and built strong stone buildings.

On the other hand, they were not necessarily healthier in the longer term. The range of ages amongst monks and the general population would have been narrower than today. People were ready victims of disease, and quite minor injuries might be fatal. With a few exceptions such as the Venerable Bede, who died at the age of 62 in 735, relatively few people would survive beyond the age of fifty. At forty they would be old people, bent with arthritis from years of living in cold damp huts.

Occasionally plays, films and television programmes have tried to show how (in the Director's vision) people lived in the past, both physically and emotionally. This is pure conjecture because of the nature of the subject, and to some historians, who have spent their painstaking lives seeking facts and evidence, it is unscientific and forbidden. But the whole idea of The Trackway of the Cross is a speculation and we hope this item will not offend those learned and disciplined experts.

A film version of Chaucer's Canterbury Tales and a television Robin Hood series were thought provoking and carried a certain imaginative weight. In these two films the usual romanticism was stripped away, the characters appeared as generally unwashed, uncouth and often on

Alan Shore plays the monk by a reconstruction of an Iron Age hut at Avoncroft Museum, Bromsgrove. This is thought to give a good impression of the type of buildings in early celtic monasteries.

(See also page 52).

the edge of lethal violence. Their lives were hard and so were they. Evidence for this view of behaviour can only come from what we know of the crowds watching a public hanging, of the popular sports such as bear baiting and cock fighting, from the pictures of Breughal and Hogarth, but such depictions seem to carry an instinctive conviction. Perhaps this is because we know that bestiality lies still below the veneer of civilisation and social order. These two films were depictions of the Middle Ages in an England where there was government and order of a sort. Imagine the Dark Ages when Roman order had gone; even when it was in place it was a very rough and violent world, with routine starvation in winter, raids and rape, killing and disease, beating of women and children.

Physical and emotional suffering might be blunted by familiarity but what would have been the mental state of people subject to constant physical and emotional battering? If they were indeed used to it, they must have lived in a different emotional condition from us. These days medicine and the law have recognised the effects of violent and disturbing incidents on accident victims, rescuers, witnesses, battered wives, soldiers, police, fire fighters and ambulance crews. Battered wives who are continuously ill treated have been found to live at a permanent high level of tension, a sort of fixed hysteria.

Any notion that the early Christian monks were meek, elderly and feeble must therefore, whatever you think of these conjectures, be quite wrong. They could not possibly have been. They were as much part of this violent society as the rest of the people, and similarly affected from birth. Imagine a young Irishman a little like one of the characters from that Robin Hood television series, a very hard, raw, young man, only basically literate but quite educated by general standards. He has found a new way of life and he wants to spread it to others and through the whole community. Perhaps part of what he has found and what he offers in his message is a break from the trauma and hysteria. He offers a new calm and mental peace - a God who is personalised, inside everyone, a source of stillness and mental order.

Inside the first little wattle and daub churches it is dark, calm and safe. When great churches and monasteries and cathedrals are later built from stone they will be oases of hallowed sanity, wombs of peace. Hypnotic chants and prayers echo in a wonderful calm space with brilliant windows. The old law of sanctuary reflects this, the holy place where the criminal could go and no violent force reach him, not even from the King. If this is what the young monk was offering then it might explain the extraordinary (and rapid) success and the civilising influence of early Christianity.

As travellers these early Christians were expert. They could navigate the sea and make a landfall in about the right spot without map or compass, in a small boat so soundly built that it could withstand Irish Sea and Atlantic storms. They could pick routes through the mountains and survive hard conditions, going everywhere on foot. Shrewd and tough, we can rely on them to be logical and efficient route makers. They would not be out to waste energy or lives on unnecessarily exposed or difficult paths, and this can add to our stock of clues.

Before going to the suggested landfall on the west coast of the Lleyn peninsula we must make one other general point. The period in question is after the Roman occupation, indeed, the events of the time might well not have occurred had there been no Roman presence or if they had not later had to withdraw. But the Romans are especially relevant because they were superb route and highway engineers. Why did the sixth century monks not follow the Roman roads, which would surely have been easier, more regular and straight, even if they had fallen into some disrepair?

The general sketch map shows the Roman Roads in North Wales, and it is obvious that none of them would have been of much help in a journey from the Lleyn Peninsula to Bangor is y coed. But why did the settlements not develop along those old roads as settlements usually do? Why did the monks not establish monasteries at points which they served?

In fact this did happen along the north coast route, or at least, the monasteries are within reach of the road. But elsewhere, and this is true of all the Celtic and later Anglo Saxon Christian settlements, the Roman achievements seem to have been almost irrelevant. The British, and later the Saxons, seemed to have had very little conception of or use for the Roman roads and the materials were often taken to build houses and churches. And for small parties on foot without wheeled vehicles, mountain paths may have been as easy travelling as the neglected Roman roads.

This raises the question of why monasteries should have been established at Clynnog Fawr on the Lleyn coast, or Bangor is y coed; neither place seems to us to be anywhere in particular. Reasons are suggested later, but we know for certain that they were in these places, and we are looking for a route between them accordingly.

Lastly, there was the problem of bands of thieves. They would naturally tend to keep watch on formal roads and it may have been safer to travel across country unobtrusively. In many ways the

Trackway of the Cross is discreet, melting into the landscape, as indeed were the early churches. A party of tough Irish monks who could sail the seas and scale mountains might well not be an easy proposition for any band of thieves, but they would be, in the early years, in small groups, and discretion would be part of their shrewdness.

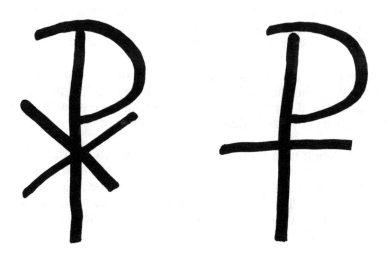

The Chi-Ro was the early Christian symbol (see page 5). The X version was the original and the cross bar a later derivative. This is the only type found in Wales and there are only two examples. See page (34) for a sketch of an inscribed gravestone at Penmachno on the Trackway.

With pagan origins and various meanings, the symbol was used in the Greek world before Christianity. It might have been adopted by Christians to disguise their affinities at times when it was dangerous. And as with many pagan institutions such as the winter and equinoctial festivals, the Chi-Ro might have been commandeered as an established and familiar symbol.

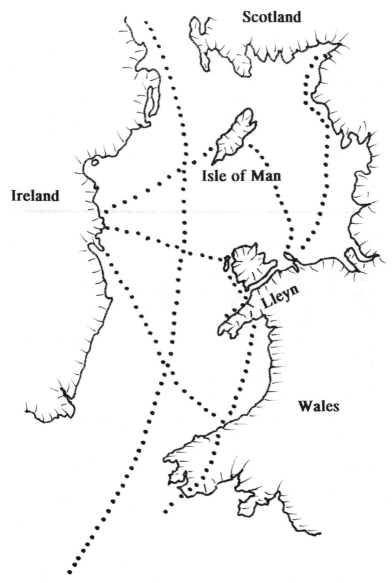

The western seaways according to Professors Fox, Bowen and Kinvig. From things found at different places it has been possible to say that travellers from the Mediterranean, Spain and Brittany sailed these routes. No doubt people also sailed from and landed at other places, but this was the the traffic which left most evidence.

Landfall

The church of St. Beuno at Clynnog Fawr was founded by the Saint in AD 630. When first built it might have had stone foundations but the rest would have been of wattle and daub or turf. Now it is an austere, remote, weatherbeaten little stone church, very handsome and well proportioned, which hangs onto a shelf of boulder clay between the open sea and the breathtaking steepness of Bwlch Mawr (509 metres) and Gyrn Goch. One wonders - why here?

Clynnog Fawr was not remote in the 5th and 6th centuries. It faced towards Ireland and civilisation, not away from it. The great monastery of Glendalough, founded by St. Kevin in AD 520 lies exactly due west over the sea and some 10 miles back from the Irish coast. Professors Kinvig and Bowen (see Reading List) consider that the Irish Sea and the Isle of Man should be regarded as a centre of Celtic christianity and of a sea transport system, this being by far the most efficient method of travelling in those days. In maps of the "Western Seaways", routes between the west coast of Britain and Ireland and the Continent, both Professors show the Isle of Man at the centre of a system, and there are indications of routes to North Wales and especially the Lleyn peninsula. Mrs Norma Lorre Goodrich in her 1986 book "King Arthur" suggests the Isle of Man as the Isle of Avalon of the Arthurian legends.

[The Irish Sea connection can be carried back into history, no doubt the seaways were used since prehistoric times. Ed]

Clynnog Fawr then, faced the "main road" and the centre of affairs rather than the reverse. Its position was relatively sheltered, or it would seem so if you had just landed on that coast in winter, and was well placed as a resting point near one of the best spots to make a landfall, or be nearly wrecked.

It is difficult to know how the coast has moved in the intervening period. The ground is boulder clay - literally, heavy clay full of enormous rocks. On the one hand the clay of a coastal strip exposed to the sea could be washed out. But once that had happened the rocks would remain to form a bank and a barrier. One could imagine the sea, after its initial success spending many hundreds of years in wearing down the rocks, and so its advance might not have been as rapid as might be supposed. This suggests that the coastline between, say Pontllyfni and Trefor, might not have changed all that much since the 6th century. The beaches in this area (where there are beaches) are shingle backed with steep clay cliffs and most of the coastline consists of cliffs of varying heights with very small beaches. To the south of Trefor the cliffs become very much higher and steeper, whilst to the north the coast tends to flatten out. It may be that the coastline has moved back but retained its general character.

Sailing in small boats from Ireland, the monks would want a landing point near St Beuno's church which they could recognise, even in bad weather, and on which it would be fairly safe to run aground, or get wrecked. The shelving shingle beach of Aberdesach, and perhaps we can assume a somewhat similar beach in the past, seems ideal by these criteria. Today its northern end is marked by a big rounded pyramid of a boulder on the point called Trwyn maen dylan, but we cannot really suggest that it has been squatting there since the 600's. The beach stretching south towards Clynnog is about half a mile long. Further to the north and the south the cliffs are steeper and the beaches either non existent or of little depth. Finally, there is a gigantic landmark in the form of the steep volcanic mountains known by the English as "The Rivals", but really named after the highest peak in the centre Yr Eifl. This chain of hills is one of the most striking and distinctive in Wales. Any resident or visitor knows it is also a prominent landmark for the Lleyn Peninsula to the south west. Seeing it on their starboard side, sea travellers would know it was time to make for the shore and look out for Trwyn maen dylan.

Grounding on the shingle, the monks would haul up their boat to rest amongst the sea holly, daisies, thorn and gorse. Around Maen Dylan they would meet cormorants, perched on rocks, diving, or beating steadily across the waves on low level fish reconnaissance. Grey seals wallow and turn by the cliffs. Splashing between the big stones and seaweed, they would walk along the sand to cross the little river Desach, the course of which must have moved up and down the beach several times since. Meeting the cliffs at the south end of the beach they must have walked along the edge for the mile or so to Clynnog.

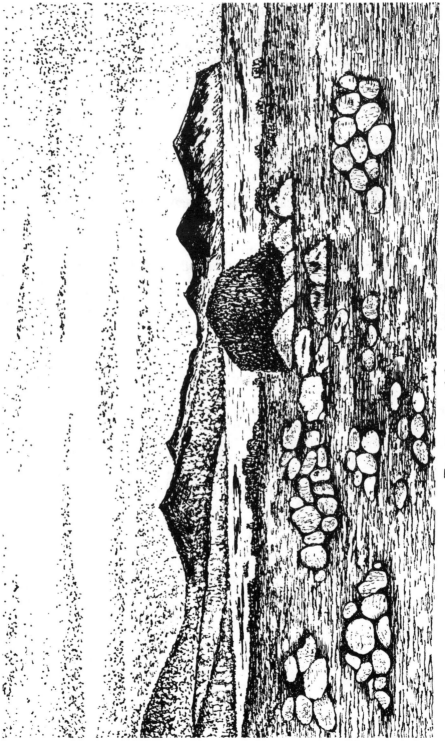

Trwyn-maen-dylan and Yr Eifl.

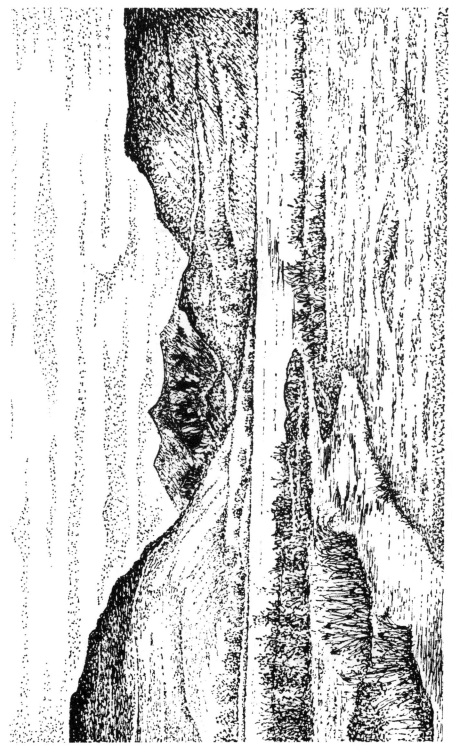

Yr Wyddfa (Snowdon) across Llyn Nantlle.

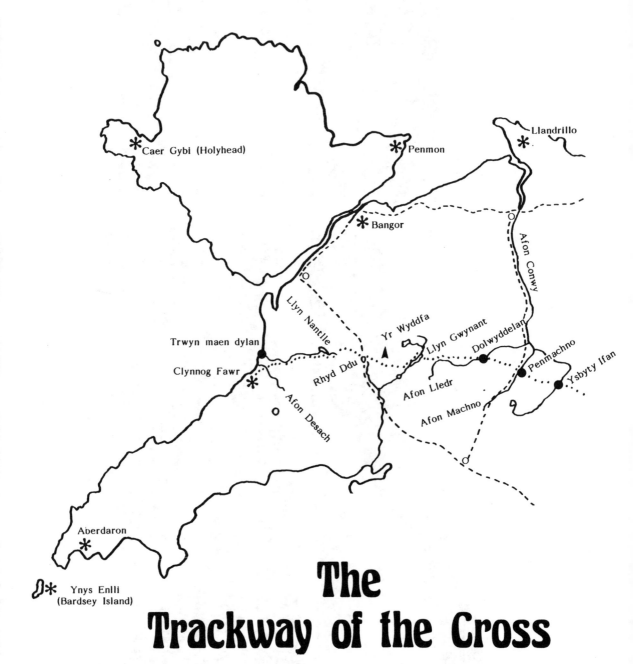

The Trackway of the Cross

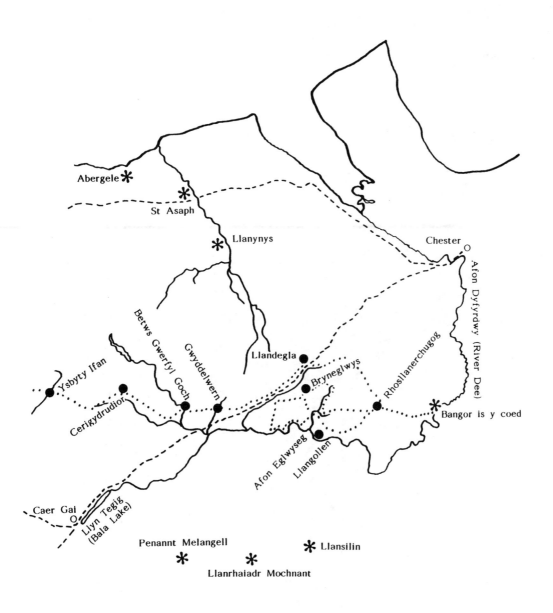

Abergele ✳

St Asaph ✳

Llanynys ✳

Chester O

Afon Dyfyrdwy (River Dee)

Betws Gwerfyl Goch

Gwyddelwern

Ysbyty Ifan ●

Cerigydrudion

Llandegla ●

Bryneglwys ●

Rhosllanerchugog

Bangor is y coed ✳

Afon Eglwyseg

Llangollen ●

Caer Gai O

Llyn Tegig (Bala Lake)

Penannt Melangell

✳
Llanrhaiadr Mochnant

✳ Llansilin

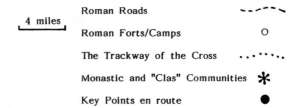

4 miles

Roman Roads

Roman Forts/Camps   O

The Trackway of the Cross

Monastic and "Clas" Communities ✳

Key Points en route   ●

(23)

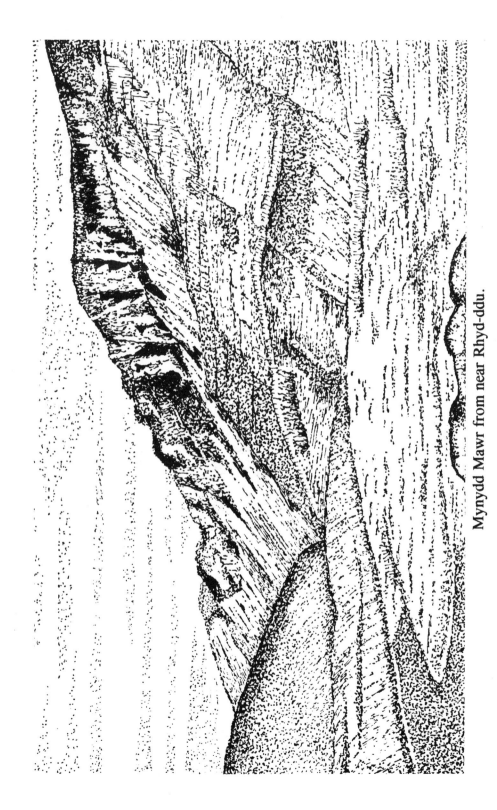

Mynydd Mawr from near Rhyd-ddu.

Clynnog Fawr to Rhyd Ddu

A journey east to Bangor is y coed can only have one immediate destination - Llyn Nantlle and the pass to Rhyd Ddu. From Clynnog Fawr lies a line through a nearby hill called Foel at 221 metres on which there is an Iron Age multivallate fort called Craig y Dinas. The line continues to Y Garn, a peak at 634 metres on Mynyth Drws Coed, which forms the southern wall of the pass leading to Rhyd Ddu.

To Nantlle, you can almost follow a straight line on foot, making the choice of whether to pass north or south of Foel. A lane passes on its north side suggesting a well established route. Small rounded hills with limestone outcrops sit between patches of grass and reeds, there are many small streams and wet areas. Poor soil and exposure mean there are few trees. The lane follows a very slight ridge and avoids the wet areas towards Llanllyfni and Pen y groes, which makes it a leading candidate as a route.

From here the monks would be in the mouth of the Nantlle valley and could walk through the foothills of the mountains to the south, avoiding marshes around the Afon Llyfni. It is now a controlled and canalised little river, but the broad acres of flood plain suggest that in the past it made the valley west of the lake very marshy.

Nantlle is a quarrying village set in a ruined landscape made mysterious by dark blue slate tips. Chains of mountains of waste rock make the old landscape hard to imagine; there was probably coarse grassland, steep to very steep in the south. The marsh and reeds must have been bleak, but once near Llyn Nantlle the travellers would in good weather have been rewarded by one of the most splendid sights in Wales. Across the lake in the foreground and framed between the steep flanks of the mountains to the north and south, Yr Wyddfa and its two shoulders stand like a crown.

The monks seem likely to have skirted the south side of Llyn Nantlle, there would be no point in crossing the Llyfni, and made their way up the valley. The grassland is gradually squeezed into the pass between the elephantine bulk of Mynyth Mawr to the north and Mynyth Drws Coed to the south.

The pass becomes high and bleak but there is no doubting the route. Once over the top at 238 metres, the valley begins to open out. A little south is Llyn y Gadair, which might have been larger or smaller than it is now, but which must have created a considerable area of marshland. The monks must have kept to the edge of the hills as the modern road does, to arrive at the Afon Gwyrfai.

From Clynog the Trackway heads for the pass to the east.

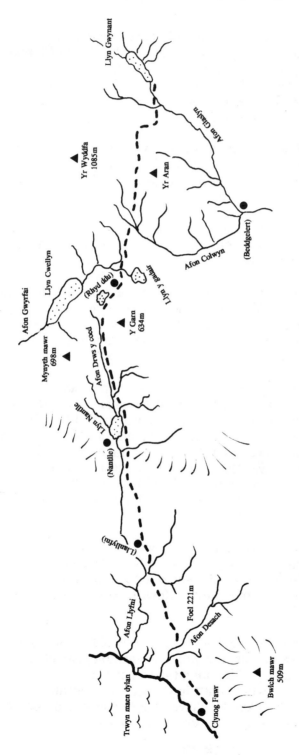

We have shown no modern roads though in places the Trackway follows their line. The names of modern towns and villages appear in brackets, just to help you orientate yourself.

Most rivers are shown because they have visibly affected the line of the route and the tributaries help to suggest the slopes. Summits appear but not contours as they would confuse the maps. On this map we have sketched in the mountain wall of the Snowdon masiff.

Yr Aran across Llyn Gwynant.

Afon Conwy at Ysbytty Ifan.

(28)

Rhyd Ddu to Llyn Gwynant

The Gwyrfai is small here since its source is Llyn y Gadair, and its valley just steep enough to make a good crossing without marshes. To the east is the peak of Yr Aran, 747 metres, providing the next sight line. Two possible routes present themselves. Either might have been used, depending on weather conditions and the season.

In summer the monks might pick their way over the upland slopes to Yr Aran to cross its north shoulder. The modern hikers path seems as likely a route as any. The path down to Nant Gwynant would probably be more or less as it is now, joining the modern Watkin Path to Yr Wyddfa and following the stream, more or less, to the Afon Glaslyn.

In severe weather the monks could have turned south east from Rhyd Ddu, followed the Nant Colwyn to its confluence with Afon Glaslyn at Beddgelert, then follow the Glaslyn north east. The valley is narrow in places, boulders and timber may have presented obstacles.

The route then lies up the valley to the head of Llyn Gwynant which might have passed on either side, searching for the steep climb to Bwlch Ehediad on the east side.

Llyn Gwynant to Ysbyty Ifan

This long succession of valleys and passes can be treated as one because it is the only part of the route where we can be almost certain of the way. It feels like and makes sense as a continuous path, connecting Nant Gwynant with Celtic churches in three successive valleys separated by quite gentle upland.

The mountainside to the east of Llyn Gwynant is steep and clothed with oak. The existence of a way through to Dolwyddelan is not obvious from the valley floor, but may have been marked by a path from prehistoric times. Quite simply, this route is the shortest safest crossing of the mountain wall between Pen y gwryd to the north and Blaenau Ffestiniog in the south.

This is the "Ancient Track" shown on an old Bartholomews map which first suggested the existence of an east west route, and it runs from Nant Gwynant to Dolwyddelan. After the first section the path is waymarked by the local council. The continuation to Penmachno is similarly marked, and the rest to Ysbytty Ifan is either a track or a lane.

The Trackway leading east across the valleys of
the Lledr, Machno and Conwy.

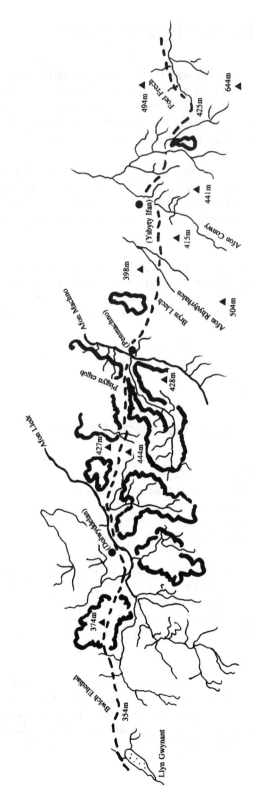

The woodlands are mainly conifer plantations but just west of
Dolwyddelan is some oak. The mass of tiny streams entering
the Lledr drain a big wet plateau.

(30)

The route is easy to walk but only moderately clear because of unfortunate gaps in waymarking, but the Walkways guide, "Bala to Snowdon" gives detailed help in both directions.

The ascent from the lake is steep and might have been more wooded for the monks; it is a muddy climb but not difficult. Quite suddenly at a height of about 200 metres you leave trees and the valley. Passing between low hills you reach an exposed moor covered in coarse grass. The ground falls falls at first to a system of marshy little streams but there are no obstacles. Then it rises steadily to enter a modern conifer forest and cross a summit at 374 metres.

The downslope through woodland begins quite steep. As it levels towards the valley floor the landscape becomes a little softer, oakwoods reappear and good grass, leading down to stone paving slabs which mark the rest of the path to the Roman Bridge.

Here the Trackway crosses the Roman road, Sarn Helen. Running north it joined the valley of the Conwy and the Chester to Bangor road, and went south to Tomen y mur by modern Trawsfynydd lake , on the Caernarfon to Caer gai road.

The monks might have crossed the Afon Lledr at this point but their ancient church at Dolwyddelan is on the north side of the river. Grassy groves of oak hang over the water and like the path approaching the bridge, the path on the south side is paved.

Dolwyddelan church stands in the centre of this wide upland valley. Today it is surrounded by buildings, but a famous watercolour in the Fitzwilliam Museum, Cambridge by Paul Sanby "Haymaking at Dolwythelan" painted in the late 1700's, shows the church and just a couple of cottages. Perhaps this gives some impression of what it looked like long ago, alone in the valley bottom against the grim pyramid of Moel Siabod (872 metres).

In about AD 600 the monk Gwyddelan - "the little Irishman" set up his preaching cross on a low hill called Bryn y bedd about 300 yards from the church. A nearby house is called Bod y groes (place of the cross). The first church was probably timber and turf and stood on Bryn y bedd. In the 12th century this was replaced by a stone building, which was demolished in 1500 and rebuilt on the present site, using some of the old materials and fittings.

A cast bronze celtic bell known as Cloch Wyddelan (Gwyddelan's bell) hangs in the nave. Unearthed from the site of the old church in 1850, it might date from the 7th century and could have been brought by the saint from Ireland.

From "Haymaking at Dolwydelan" by Paul Sandby,
probably late eighteenth century.

(32)

The way to Penmachno involves climbing out of the valley of the Lledr, crossing a pass (Bwlch y groes) at about 360 metres between hills of 444 and 427 metres, and dropping down to the Afon Machno.

At Dolwyddelan a valley enters that of the Lledr from the south and it seems the natural escape route. But it is a closed valley with very steep sides and just a couple of miles long. Instead the route takes a steep but easier climb up the tumbling stream of the Afon Bwlch y groes. Winding upwards through oakwoods you join a track beside a modern conifer forest, which was probably grass moor in the 6th century. The trees end a little short of the crest of the pass, and the monks would have made a straight line over a hilly moor of grass and heather.

The crest of the first rise is followed by a short uneven plateau ending at the little hill known as Pisgyn Esgob, which means bishop's mitre. Since it looks a little like one this may have some or no significance.

From the Pisgyn the modern walker enters young conifers. The ground is marshy and may have been more so before the trees were planted. However this is only for a half mile or so, and a modern lane falls steeply to the village of Penmachno.

The old church here was founded by St Tudclud in 540, and he is said to have been trained in the priesthood at Bangor is y Coed, all of which is inferred from some Latin inscribed stones on the site.

Rising south east from the village and the valley of the Machno is a wide bare hillside with a gradual slope. The fields have stone walls and it is noticeably less wild then the exit from the valley of the Lledr.

A modern lane leads straight up to two little farms at 297 metres which sit at the base of the last rise to the summit. A steep rocky track, which may not have been much different for the monks, reaches a crest at 400 metres. But the landscape confirms its new and gentler character, being rounded rather than jagged.

The track drops gradually to a stream at Pontrhydyrhalen (bridge of the salt ford). Minerals give the water a sinister brown tint and the waterside grasses look sickly.

The track now becomes a surfaced lane, not in good repair, which crosses the Afon Eidda and rises gently to the last crest before Ysbytty Ifan. The lane bends west to make an easy slope to the valley floor, but by taking a gate on the left just as the lane starts to fall, you can follow an old route. Deep between earth banks with rock underfoot is a dark moist tunnel under the trees. Meeting a farm track it drops to the B4407 at Ysbytty Ifan beside some alms cottages.

Ysbytty Ifan means John's Hospice (Ysbytty is modern Welsh for hospital) and was built on the site of the present church by the Knights of St John in about 1120. Today there is just a pretty hamlet with a sturdy stone bridge over the young Afon Conwy, a chapel and a Post Office. The village is about half way between Clynnog Fawr and Bangor is y coed, but if this alone seems insufficient reason for founding a hospice, the valley of the Conwy gives access to the north and the coastal monasteries of Llandrillo and Abergele. Ysbytty Ifan was therefore at a junction.

Whether the monks would have had any interest in travelling south is more doubtful. Once out of the Conwy Valley they would have had to cross the truly awful moor called the Migneint, and settlements to the south would have been better reached by going south from Penmachno.

✲ ✲ ✲

"Carausius lies here in this heap of stones."
Grave stone with Chi-Ro at Penmachno church,
5th or early 6th century.

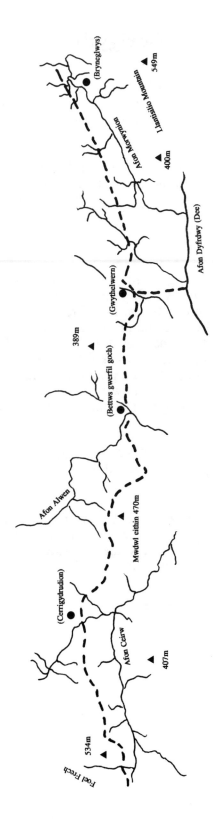

The ridge from Foel Frech avoids the marshes. The lanes and tracks between Cerrigydrudion and Gwythelwern suggest a continuous way, which continues north east.

From Gwythelwern a possible alternative route for the monks is shown heading south. If the Dyfrdwy (Dee) was navigable by (say) coracles from the Corwen area it would give a fast and easy passage to Bangor is y coed.

Ysbyty Ifan to Cerigydrudion

Looking east from Ysbytty Ifan there is no absolutely clear track
that we can point to as the only likely way to Bangor is y coed.
However, the lie of the land and the immediate destination do
suggest a highly probable route.

Cerigydrudion seems likely to have been the next destination, where
yet another church was founded in the 6th century. It stands on a
small hill at the eastern end of the valley of the Afon Ceirw before
it turns south. This east west section is marshy in spite of modern
drainage and you can imagine the valley being a difficult place in
the past.

East from Ysbytty Ifan, a lane suggests the route. The ground rises
quickly to upland hills, wide and sweeping rather than steep. The
obvious target would have been the pass at Foel Frech (425 metres)
to which a green track runs after the end of the surfaced lane.
The main danger would have been marshes near the streams between
them, this is a high rainfall area, and the track follows a stream
for nearly a mile. The pass is one of those grand watersheds, for
the streams behind flow north into the Conwy and the Irish Sea,
whereas those ahead flow south into the Dee, and ultimately of
course, the Irish Sea again.

The steep sided narrow valley of the Afon Ceirw leads on. Soft reedy
patches which quickly develop beside it could be avoided by walking
on the north side of the valley.

After a mile and a half is a place called Pengwern, head of the
marsh. No doubt the monks would have swung a little further north to
avoid it entirely and followed the broad whaleback ridge between Moel
Eglwys and Cerigydrudion, where there is now a lane.

Cerigydrudion to Bryneglywys

Contours on this section are steep but not rugged; upland hills but
not mountains. The highest point is Mwdwl eithin at 470 metres.
The heights of the hill tops to the east reduce steadily. Bryneglwys
stands on a prominent hill quite distinctly above the valley in
which it sits, but at only 228 metres. These days the grassland has
been enclosed, reseeded and tamed. But even in the past the uneven
and boggy grass moors would have been friendly compared with the
mountains.

The general direction is almost a straight line east through Betws
gwerfyl goch and Gwyddelwern where there are 6th century churches,
to Bryneglwys where there is another.

From Cerigydrudion a lane runs south east past an Iron Age hillfort
called Caer Caradog (Caradoc seems to have had more forts that the
US Cavalry) which suggests the approach to the small mountain of
Mwdwl eithin. Then a track shown on modern maps leads over the
north shoulder. Several descents are possible to Betws gwerfyl
goch but perhaps the monks would have avoided the northern section
of the steep deep Alwen valley, which might have been an overgrown
tangle.

Betws church was founded by St Beuno and nearby is a holy well.
Similarly at Gwyddelwern, reached by a steep climb from the Alwen to
cross the southern slopes of Mynydd rhyd ddu, perhaps on the line of
the modern lane.

There is no single obvious route towards Bryneglwys but there are no
particular obstacles and a variety of ways. The Roman road from Caer
gai to Chester (now the A5104) is quite likely. It is easily reached
from Gwyddelwern and forms the natural route up the valley of the
Afon Morwynion.

Bryneglwys (church on a hill) was founded by St Tysilio on the "bryn"
in AD 575. The first church was of turf and wattle and not much above
ground level. A second church of boulders was built around the site
of the first and some of them are now in the west wall of the present
church (built 1570 and 1872).

St Tysilio's Church at Bryneglwys.

The Trackway from
Bryneglywys to Bangor is y coed

The Trackway so far was surveyed by John Roberts in 1987, but ten years earlier I had involved another friend, also younger and more active than me, in the search for a route east from Bryneglwys. Where the monks might have gone from there is a speculation which most people seem to agree would involve settling for one, or all, of several possible alternatives.

This section after Gwyddelwern has no obvious connection in a straight line either with Bangor is y coed or Valle Crucis Abbey, though both are near a west east alignment on the map. Physically two great masses intervene, the Llantysillio and Ruabon Mountains. These are separated by the deep valley of the Eglwyseg River and bounded on their flanks to the south by the contortions of the River Dee in the Vale of Llangollen.

[Possibly, but only possibly, from Gwyddelwern the monks might have sailed down the Afon Dyfrdwy (Dee). Coracles are still used in some parts of Wales and would probably have been available locally. They are designed to be carried and there is easy access south to the river at Corwen. Severe rapids before Glyndyfrdwy might have presented a problem, but should not rule out this route. Coracles are light and handy for shallow water and easily portaged round obstructions, much as modern conoeists carry their craft round canal and river locks. Ed]

In the centre of the ridge of the Llantysilio Mountains is the second Bwlch y Groes. *[bwlch = pass. Ed.]* The 53rd degree of Latitude runs just a short distance south of Gwyddelwern through this bwlch over the Ruabon Mountain near Pen y Cae, and practically aligns with the straight road running into Bangor, the site of the great early monastery called by Bede, Bancornaburg, also on the 53rd parallel; a fitting termination for the "Trackway of the Cross".

[There is a straight line route from the Eglwyseg valley to Bangor which Alan seems to have missed. I explain later. Ed]

However, although there are these map alignments there is no straight way on the ground. The Eglwyseg Rocks are a formidable barrier to travel and while an active man might find somewhere to scale them, certainly it would be an unacceptable route for regular journeying. However, in an age before roads fit for wheeled vehicles existed, with no bridges over main rivers, dependent on fords and when swamps and scrubby woods filled the valleys, there must have been at least one high level route.

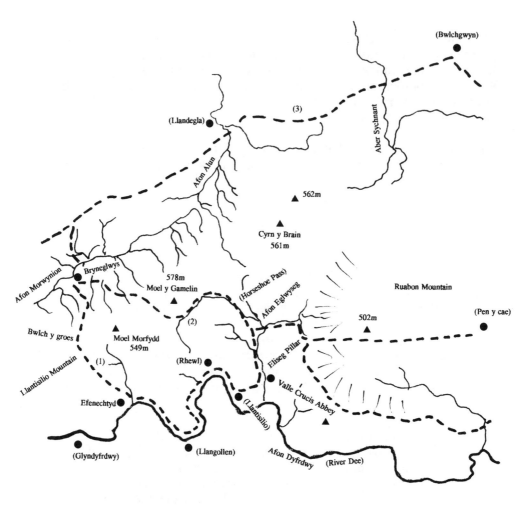

(Bwlchgwyn)

(3)

Aber Sychnant

(Llandegla)

Afon Alun

▲ 562m

▲
Cyrn y Brain
561m

Bryneglwys

578m
Moel y Gamelin
▲

(Horseshoe Pass)

Afon Eglwyseg

Ruabon Mountain

Afon Morwynion

(2)

502m
▲

(Pen y cae)

Bwlch y groes

Moel Morfydd
549m
▲

Eliseg Pillar

Llantisilio Mountain

(1)

(Rhewl)

Valle Crucis Abbey

Efenechtyd

(Llantisilio)
▲

(Glyndyfrdwy)

(Llangollen)

Afon Dyfrdwy   (River Dee)

(1) River Route
(2) Mountain Route
(3) Ridgeway Route

Bryneglywys to Bangor is y coed

(40)

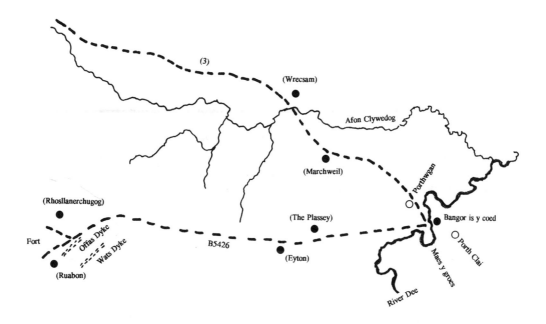

We have shown as many names as possible but tried
not to clutter the map. The spelling may differ
from that used by Alan Shore and Leonard Sanders,
but we have tried to give current versions.

Because I could not determine any even likely route across this section, I started at the other end, i.e. at Bangor, along that road west and viewed from there, remembered there was a notch in the skyline. This was about 280 degrees grid West, presumably near Rhosllanerchrugog, which looked as if access to Ruabon Mountain there might be easy. I had not been up and so had not myself been able to test if there is any corresponding way on the west side through the Eglwyseg Rocks.

By 1982 I had come to the conclusion that I was placing too much importance on a straight track on the ground, whereas the value of the Ley was to determine direction. It was time therefore to get a fresh mind on the investigation, free from ley obsession. Accordingly I asked a very old friend for help. This was Leonard Sanders who knew this part of North Wales well by frequently walking over it. He volunteered to sort out the section from Gwyddelwern and in June 1982 he sent me a sketch map with carefully detailed reports of three feasible routes. Not one is straight but no river has to be crossed and the proposed tracks are on high ground and keep to the desired direction wherever possible. Here are Leonard's reports:

* * * * *

21st June 1982

Dear Alan,

During the last few months I have been rewalking the mountain area through which your ancient missionaries must have travelled on that section of their journey terminating between Bryn Eglwys and Bangor is y Coed. I am therefore sure that all the details of the routes suggested are correct.

To illustrate the text I am enclosing a rough outline map to a scale of 1 in 25,000 with numbered grid lines to enable you to refer it to your own maps.

In offering three suggested routes I feel they are reasonably likely, and whilst favouring number (1), I see no reason why all three may not have been available.

On the other hand I have no evidence that any of these tracks existed during the period under consideration.

Perhaps some day we may be able to go over this terrain together.

Possible ancient routes from
Bryneglwys to Bangor is y coed.

1. THE RIVER ROUTE   Distance 20 miles

A minor road leaves Bryneglwys and climbs the western shoulder of
Moel Morfydd to a point on the map named Bwlch y groes (Pass of the
cross), on the 1350 foot contour. Several tracks descend to the
road alongside the River Dee and near to Glyndyfrdwy. *[See below my
note on the river as a route. Ed]* By following this road eastwards
for a short distance one comes to a farmhouse, "Efenechtyd". The
name is said to be derived from "y fynach ty", the Monk's House,
fynach being the soft mutation of mynach. It was possibly a monk's
cell or ysbyty where rest, food and shelter were obtainable.

Behind the farmhouse a gated public footpath climbs steadily and
leads on to open moorland over which an old track is traceable as a
hollow way, though now it is criss crossed by sheep tracks. The path
then descends to the road again above another farmhouse named "Groes
Llwyd" (The Grey Cross or Lloyd's Cross). This path saves a mile
over the road and is easier going.

The route then follows the road along the river valley through the
hamlet of Rhewl and the village of Llantysilio. Just before
Llantysilio Farm a narrow lane to the left leads to the main
Horseshoe Pass Road up which it is necessary to walk to the next turn
to the right dipping down to the confluence of Afon Eglwyseg and the
Pentredwr Brook, until about 1930 crossed by a ford.

This lane joins the narrow road coming down from World's End which
takes the traveller close along the foot of the Eglwyseg and Trevor
Rocks to the end of the Vale of Llangollen and so to Bangor is y
coed.

*[Here I mention the river route again. If rapids between Corwen and
Glyndyfrdwy would have prevented navigation by coracles and
portaging was not possible, the Afon Dyfrdwy becomes much easier from
Glyndyfrdwy. And it would have carried them straight to their
destination.*

*The Eliseg Pillar (see Alan's later comments), and the ruins of Vale
Crucis Abbey are about 400 yards apart and both near the point where
the lane from Llantisilio Farm joins the Horseshoe Pass road. The
Abbey was founded in 1201, but some connection with the Trackway is
suggested later. Ed.]*

2. THE MOUNTAIN ROUTE   Distance 17 miles

From Bryneglwys a narrow but negotiable road leads eastward along the
northern flanks of Moel Morfydd and Moel Gamelyn, climbing steadily
until it joins the main Llangollen-Ruthin Road at the head of the
Horseshoe Pass, 1300 feet. It passes the slate quarries and must
have been used by quarrymen, though this does not preclude an earlier
origin.

From this point it is an old road signposted as "The Old Horseshoe
Pass" which descends quickly straight down to the village of
Pentredwr to join the route described in (1).

*[In the great wall of limestone that bands the western flank of the
Ruabon Mountain and forms the east side of the Eglwyseg Valley,
there are two interesting looking gaps. Both are accessible from the
lane which Leonard describes as leading from World's End and past
Trevor Rocks. From one a footpath leads directly across the moor to
Pencae. When considering possible routes to Bangor Alan noted a deep
nick in the skyline of Ruabon Mountain, and this is where the path
emerges. So this is another possible route although perhaps not a
good one in winter. Ed.]*

3. THE RIDGEWAY ROUTE   Distance 20 miles

A minor road, having all the characteristics of an ancient ridgeway,
runs from Gwyddelwern, passing a little to the north of Bryneglwys,
and joins the modern Corwen to Pen y ffordd road a few yards to the
west of the crossing with the Llangollen to Ruthin road.

From there it is a short distance downhill to the village of
Llandegla (Church of St. Tegla) and St. Tegla's Well, for many years
a resting place for cattle drovers on their way from Angelsey and
North Wales to London. The old drovers' track is still traceable for
a short distance but has mostly been absorbed by road construction in
the area of Minera, Bersham and Wrexham.

If, as is possible, it was based on an earlier track it could have
connected thence with a route to Bangor is y coed.

*[The modern A525 to Bwlchgwyn then south east through Wrecsam is a
possible line, and it runs straight to Bangor is y coed. It would
involve crossing the Afon Clywedog. Ed]*

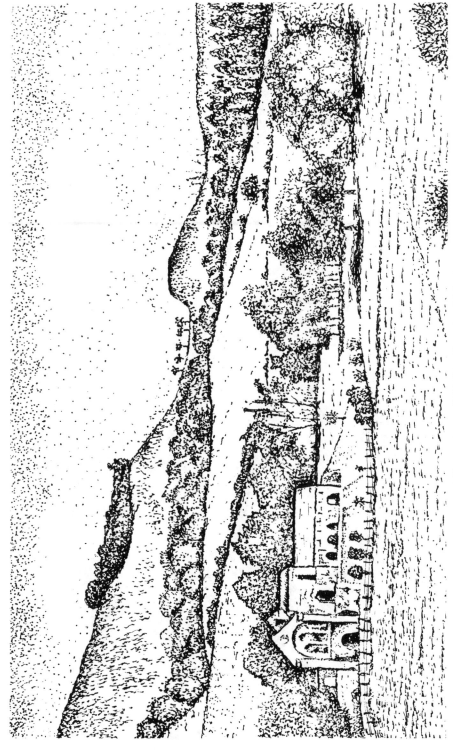

The ruins of Valle Crucis Abbey.

The break in the limestone wall of the Ruabon Mountain from the Eglwyseg Valley.

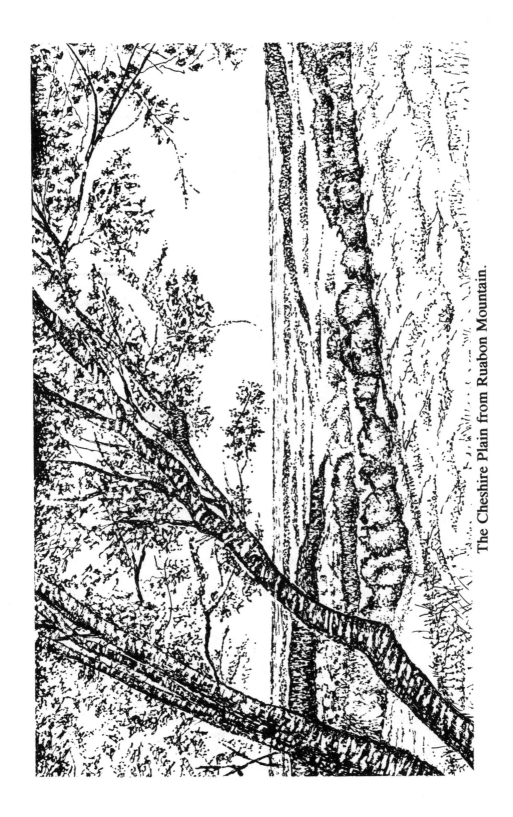

The Cheshire Plain from Ruabon Mountain.

NOTES

The River Route passes through three places having names of monastic association, Bwlch y groes, Efenechtyd and Groes Llwyd, giving support to the claim that they were used by monks and missionaries.

Whilst the Ridgeway Route avoids crossing the mountain range into the Vale of Llangollen it does rise to 1300 feet. I have known snow to drift deep and lie long on the higher section, so that it may not have offered better winter travelling than the other routes.

The first two routes described offer some fine mountain walking, passing through ever changing scenery.

I have often wondered why George Borrow's guide, honest John Jones, did not take the Old Horseshoe Pass Road when they walked from Llangollen to Ruthin and back in the day. ["Wild Wales" - published 1855] It would have saved them several miles of tedious walking.

L.S. June 1982

[John Jones may have been honest but George Borrow was a romancer with very optimistic views about the distances he walked. Ed]

* * * * *

Like Leonard, I prefer his No.1 River Route, especially as it has the Efenechtyd or "Monks' House" on it. But if ROUND the south of the Ruabon Mountain is the ONLY way, I am still at a loss why the straight road from Bangor sets out almost due west as if there were a route OVER the mountain. It is true this peters out after the Fox public house and it is now crossed first by Wat's and then by Offa's Dykes.

[The footpath over the mountain continues Alan's straight line. Ed]

Bangor under the wood was established before the Battle of Chester AD 616 and the dykes are years later (Offa's c.780). It is natural therefore that the way hereabouts should have become confused because after c.780 direct communication with Ireland would be broken. From the mouth of the Vale of Llangollen, or somewhere on a line due north of there, depending upon which approach they took, the monks would head for Bangor is y coed by the most direct line.

Small hills rise at the foot of Ruabon Mountain but soon vanish. This landscape is more typical of England than Wales as it slopes gradually to the Dee. Marshes probably started at the flood plain of the river near modern Eyton. Maps show a suggestive windmill, possibly water pump, at the Plassey. The travellers would no longer face the problems of exposure, but some new ones. This well wooded landscape suggests an even denser past and would have formed the edge of the great Midland forests. Dense woodland can be extremely difficult to navigate, straight lines are impossible because of undergrowth, landmarks are few and one glade or path can look much like another. And it changes constantly, trees fall, growth disguises tracks.

On the whole there seems no reason to disagree with the general line suggested by the modern B5426 from Johnstown at the foot of the Ruabon mountain to Eyton *[This is an 18th century toll road but might well have been laid on a slight natural ridge. Ed.]* East of this the monks would probably have had to keep such dry ground as there was and a selection of meandering tracks.

Bangor is y coed

Bangor is y coed, or Bangor on Dee as the English have it, is a quiet unremarkable commuter village on the east bank of the river. The Dee winds and twists past between deep clay banks, resembling more an intestine than a river as it rambles across its flood plain. Bangor has an attractive eighteenth century church, but it has nothing whatever to do with ancient monks and trackways, because the point of interest is thought to lie on the opposite bank of the Dee.

Bangor is y coed appears on the Dark Ages Map; it is recorded also in the "Historical Atlas of Wales" by William Rees, as one of the Mother Churches of Wales in the eighth to eleventh centuries. The name means "the Monastery under the Wood" and it dates from the middle of the sixth century. It was founded by St Deiniol (or Daniel) who established the other Bangor in Arfon. The actual site of the monastery has not yet been determined by any ground evidence. As long ago as 1775 Thomas Pennant wrote in "A Tour of Wales", the first of his three volume record of "Home Travels": "I could discover no remains of this once noted place; but was informed that square stones have been often ploughed up in a field called "Stanyards", *[Stoneyards. Ed.]* probably the site of some of the ancient buildings."

Pennant also quotes from William of Malmsbury, contemporary with King Stephen (1135-54): "no place could show greater remains of half demolished churches and multitudes of other remains that were to be seen in his time. Mention is made of two gates of the precincts, that were a mile distant, with the Dee running between them; one was called "Porth Clais", the other "Porth Wgan". *[Porth = gate. Ed]* The name of the first is retained in that of a place called "Clai"; of the other in a house called "Hogan". "Bartholomew's 1/2" map used "Porth y gan" formerly but changed it in 1964 to "Porthwgan". Pennant said of Bangor: "The church has been built at different times; but no part very ancient. It is a rectory dedicated to St. Dinoth (Bede calls him Dinoct) abbot of Bancornaburg or Bangor, in the days of St. Augustine."

About two miles to the east is Worthenbury and a similar distance to the north west is Marchwiel, both with dedications to St. Deiniol; a fact which seems to show Bangor had a wide influence in the neighbourhood.

After I had written this, just before my talk of 1972, I bought an Ordnance Survey 2.5 inch map, sheet SJ34 Wrecsam South, but did not examine it closely. Then later I found: a patch of ground bounded on the west, north and east by a bend of the Dee and on the north by the straight road from Bangor is y coed bridge. It is plainly marked GROES and just across the river, to the east is MAES Y GROES the "Field of the Cross", a fitting termination for "The Trackway of the Cross."

The monastery probably lay in a contortion of the river which almost creates an island, and is today as short of interest as any other score of acres of winter barley. Nothing marks it as the destination of an Ancient Trackway. But this is not surprising, for a glance at the O.S. Dark Ages Map confirms that there were few centres of population then and practically no places of national importance as judged by present day standards; so that when an ancient trackway is suspected, it is of little use looking for a town, say, as its source or its destination.

What is significant is that Groes, traditional site of the monastery, is on the Welsh side of the Dee, confirming that communication was with the WEST and a wide river did not have to be crossed.

[The line of a Roman road has lately been discovered running from the Wrecsam/Chester area to Hanmer a few miles south east of Bangor is y coed. It passed through both gates of the monastery and therefore crossed the Dee more or less at the modern bridge. There seems to be no evidence of any Roman structure, which would have needed to be substantial, so perhaps there was a ford or a ferry.

River Dee and presumed site of the monastery at Bangor-is-y-coed, "as short of interest as any other score of acres of winter barley".

However, the Roman crossing and the fact of the two gates to the monastery suggests that crossing the Dee at this point was not such a problem as Alan thought. Could some sort of crossing have been a reason for its location? Ed.}

In September 1972, after I had visited the neighbouring parish church at Marchwiel, the Rev. D. Saunders Davies wrote to me to say "It may interest you to know that the two old words that make up the name Marchwiel are still in use in rural parts of Wales. "March" is the Welsh name for a stallion and when used as an adjective means "sturdy". "Wiel" comes from "Gweail" which means "withies" or "wattle". It is generally believed that the first church in our valley was built of wattle and daub and it is my guess that any buildings that housed the monks of Bangor must have been of the same material."

Then in November 1982, I was in correspondence with Mr. Christopher Taylor, one of Britain's best known archaeologists and a member of the Royal Commission on Historical Monuments. He is the author of "Roads and Tracks of Britain" (published in 1979). I sent him a photograph of a reconstruction of some Iron Age buildings which had been erected at Avoncroft near Bromsgrove (a museum of buildings), at that time, together with me in a brown robe being a monk (picture page 13). The scene was of a few timber and thatch hutments within a wattle fence, and Mr. Taylor confirmed it "was exactly what a Celtic monastery must have looked like". And he said "I always find it difficult to get over to people this fact. The popular idea of a monastery is always one of the great medieval buildings."

We know from reports of the Battle of Chester (615) from various sources, particularly Bede, that there was a large self supporting Celtic community at Bangor in the seventh century. He says (II.2) King Aethelfrith made a great slaughter of the "faithless Britons", for about 1200 monks who had come from Bangor to pray for the British cause were put to death as a preliminary to the fighting. He adds that "the monastery held so many monks that, although it was divided into seven sections each under its own abbot, none of these sections contained less than 300 monks." This means then there was a total of at least 2100 men there.

Bangor must have been literally "under the wood", for there are many "wood" names on the map and numerous meres and patches of fen still dot the flat low lying lands east of the River Dee. The forest proper started probably at Threapwood, an Anglo Saxon name. Three miles east is Sarn Bridge indicating, by its Celtic name, that there was a "paved way" there before the Saxon occupation.

Bangor was a far outpost of the Celtic Church; it was far enough east to be on the English side when Offa built his Dyke in the eighth century. Before this contact was to the west with Ireland, and to the east, so far as the British were concerned, was jungle and the savages.

It is not surprising that there is now no trace of the original monastery for it was undoubtedly built of wood; a number of huts were enclosed by a wattle fence. Traditionally the name "Bangor" has been derived from "ban": high or lofty, and "cor": a choir. Now it is considered that it signifies the enclosing fence - "bangor" being "the binding part" of a wattle fence (History of Wales, by Sir John E. Lloyd).

There is a tradition that soon after the Battle of Chester the surviving monks from Bangor decamped to Bardsey. At any rate the island was supposed to be the resting place of 20,000 saints and in the Middle Ages it became the goal of very many pilgrims as an object of great veneration - two such journeys were then held to equal one trip to Rome. However, it is likely that the monastery did survive for some time yet; for when Bede wrote about it in AD 731 he gave it the English name of Bancornaburg, implying that at that time the English border was not far from the Dee.

By the late eighth century what was once all Britain now became the separate countries of England and Wales and Bangor found itself on the English side of the newly built dikes: Wat's and Offa's. Thus contact with Ireland or Gaul and the West via the Trackway would be broken, and the eastern section certainly would quickly fall into disuse. This may in part explain what we have already noted: there is a straight road running directly west, for several miles, from the Dee bridge at Bangor but there is no continuation in this direction once Wat's Dike is encountered.

[I have noted that the direct road (B5426) is an 18th century toll road, but might well have been built upon a slight natural ridge. Alan was not aware that from just south of this road a link between the two dikes has been traced. A (possibly) prehistoric trackway runs between them and on to the ancient Ruabon hillfort. This would be consistent with both Leonard Sanders first and second routes and the track over Ruabon Mountain from the Elwyseg Valley. Ed]

Notes and Comments

Annals

Welsh, Irish and Anglo Saxon all record the Battle of Chester, giving dates around AD 613, which Mrs. Norah Chadwick has amended, by various calendar corrections, to AD 616. According to Bede, the Saxon leader Aethelfrith beat the Welsh and 1200 monks from Bancornaburg were slain after Bocmail, who was supposed to protect them, left them to their fate.

In Welsh and Irish records under various forms of the name "Selim" (Solomon), a well known figure of heroic poetry and romance called in Welsh "Selyf" was also slain there. Now Selyf was son of Cynan Garwyn, son of Brochfael Ysgithrog. Norah Chadwick thinks that this Brochfael is the same "Brocmail" who led the Bangor monks and she says: "The Welsh Life of St. Beuno' written in AD 1306 and based, in its earlier part at least, on a lost Vita of earlier date, relates to Brochfael, king of Powys, and his sons and descendants; and here a close connection between Powys and Gwynedd is implicit in the story, for when the sons of Selyf treat the saint badly he makes his way to Arfon, where he is treated with respect by King Cadfan". If Norah Chadwick's contention is right that Brochfael is the same man as Brocmail, then Beuno links with Bangor is y coed as well as Clynog.

Cadfan Stone

The memorial stone to King Cadfan has already been noted when discussing the Latin cross as a Christian symbol. It is to be found at Llangadwaladr, Anglesey, about 2 m. from the two Beuno dedications of Aberffraw and Trefdraeth and midway between them. A translation of the Latin inscription reads: "King Catamanus, wisest (and) most renowned of all kings (lies here)." It is certainly strange in view of the name of our Trackway that Beuno's king should have the first Latin CROSS in Wales on his memorial stone and reliably dated by Nash Williams as AD 625 - though really just a coincidence.

Cross: y Groes

A note by Lady C. Guest in her 1877 version of Mabinogion is probably the simplest explanation of "y Groes" applied to tracks. Referring to Rhyd y Groes, near Berriew (p.322), she says: "The intersection of

The Eliseg Pillar has been vandalised by travellers and
battered by centuries of harsh weather. Knocked down by the
Parliamentary army in the Civil War, it lay on the ground
for years untill reerected in 1779.

these two roads appears to have occurred at no great distance from the ford which doubtless derived its distinctive appellation of y Groes either from this circumstance, or from the Rood or Cross often set up both in crossways and upon the margins of fords."

The Eliseg Pillar

The pillar stands in the Eglwyseg valley near the site of Valle Crucis Abbey. It was erected by Cyngen, great grandson of Eliseg who was the last ruler of the kingdom of Powys. He died in AD 854 so the pillar had nothing to do with the Trackway of the Cross. It is however an interesting monument and it does not seem unreasonable to suppose that such a memorial would have been placed on or near to a well used route for travellers to see.

[The Eglwyseg Valley is a northward exit from the central Vale of Llangollen. Ed]

Ireland Bangor Sea Route

Bangor is y coed is on the bank of the River Dee, a good sized river and not very far in those days from open water at Chester. (The estuary did not begin to assume its present silted up state until the mid 15th century.) And although a glance at the river's course on a map shows almost insane contortions just north of Bangor, so that no vessel of any size could navigate it, in small coracle type craft the river might be a speedy and effortless way to the sea. It might be argued that the route to Ireland lay this way. However, I believe the original movement was FROM Ireland, starting from the coast near Clynnog Fawr. The distance across the sea from here is only about half that between Chester and Ireland; furthermore the "Trackway" would be safer, avoiding land attacks from Saxons and sea raiders round Chester and the Wirral where northern placenames are plentiful, i.e. Scandinavian: Thurstaston, Caldy, Meols - and Danish: Frankby, Kirby, Irby, Raby, though Norsemen are not actually recorded until c.850.

[I noted earlier that the Dee might well have been used from the Llangollen area. Ed]

Middle Ages

Now when we come to the Middle Ages, it is clear that the pilgrims had a ready made route right through the mountains to join the well defined "Saints' Road to Bardsey" along the west coast of Lleyn through Clynnog and Pistyll.

The eastern terminal of the Trackway at this time might well be Valle Crucis, where the Cistercian abbey, an off shoot of Strata Marcella, was founded on 28th January 1201. Round this time, or when the route became popular, the Knights Hospitallers of St. John of Jerusalem set up a hospice for pilgrims at the place still known as Yspyty Ifan. (This must have been some time after AD 1120 because the Order did not exist before that date.) It is significant that Yspyty is located on the present Ffestiniog - Denbigh road exactly where that road is crossed by the Trackway, that is about two miles south of the modern A5. I submit that this points to the fact that it was the presence of the Trackway which caused the hospice to be built, not vice versa. A shrine or even a monastery might certainly be located in an out of the way place but a hospice is not provided unless there is a need for it, that is unless there are people already travelling along a route.

Survivals and Continuity

In "Britain and the Western Seaways" 1972 Prof. E.G. Bowen, when referring to Gallo Roman Irish wanderers in the 5th and 6th centuries: "Penetration from north west Wales was impeded by the great mountain massifs and the heavily forested lowlands of the Cheshire plain that lay beyond."

By the time that this was written it had become obvious to me that Prof. Bowen's observations were only too true in this final section and establishing a straight line of practical track here might prove impossible.

The fact that survivals from widely different periods are found along a trackway does not necessarily invalidate the tracks existence; on the contrary, it can confirm it. Objects are where they are simply because the track was there already and it has been in use for a long time. So with the Trackway of the Cross there could have been continuity from the Iron Age, through the Age of Saints right to the Middle Ages.

With the building of bridges in the valleys and the construction of proper roads coupled with the decline of pilgrimages in Tudor times, though sections might survive, the Trackway as a continuous route would then cease to exist.

To conclude: There are many well defined lengths of path along "The Trackway of The Cross" and these have been of greater or less importance at different periods of its history. For instance, Fay Godwin and Shirley Toulson in their well researched book of 1977 on "The Drover's Roads of Wales" refer to tracks in use by the drovers for hundreds of years until the middle of the last century in the Penmachno and Yspyty Ifan district, and give a very detailed description of my route from Cerigydrudion through Betws Gwerfyl Goch to Gwyddelwern. However, so far I have failed to trace anyone who, say in the last thousand years, has walked all the way from the Irish Sea to Bangor is y Coed.

Appendix

University College, Cardiff Department of Archaeology
Professor R.J.C. Atkinson, M.A., F.S.A.

17 July 1974

Dear Mr. Shore,

I am sorry that it has taken me rather longer than I had hoped to write to you again about your Trackway of the Cross. I have had to be away at meetings in London and elsewhere for much of the last ten days. However I have now re-read your paper in conjunction with the relevant maps, and I think what follows is substantially what I put in my missing letter of April.

You will understand that I can claim no expertise in the archaeology of the post-Roman period; but with that proviso it seems to me that your suggested route is not merely possible but probable, and that its origins could well go back into prehistoric times, and not necessarily only to the pre-Roman Iron Age. We know, after all, that throughout the Bronze Age there was a well-established trade in bronze tools and weapons, manufactured in Ireland but used in England and Wales, and that for centres of Bronze Age population in, for instance, the southern Pennine area the routes used must have crossed north Wales from west to east. I have had a look at the distribution of bronze finds of this period in the area in question, but they are not sufficiently numerous, or sufficiently differentiated in pattern to lend any particular support to your route rather than another.

The difficulty about all this is that, unlike a made road where hypotheses about the course of a missing section can usually be checked by excavation, a putative trackway of this kind provides no real means of verification. The presence of points along it of significant monuments, such as crosses or memorial stones, cannot in general be used for this purpose, since it is these which have been chosen to define the nodes, as it were, of the route itself in the first place. This is a methodological problem which arises in all studies of early communications where no artificial construction of a road is involved, and as far as I can see it is an insoluble one. This means that one can only fall back on judgements of probability which cannot be more than subjective and personal.

As regards the way in which the route may have been marked by natural "foresights", such as notches on the skyline, I can see no difficulty, because what you suggest is open to none of the very real objections that can be levelled at the "old straight track" theory of Alfred Watkins. Those objections, as you are clearly aware, arise partly from his insistence that the "tracks" were straight lines (though in fact, of course, most of his straight lines drawn ON THE MAP are necessarily curved ON THE GROUND, because the map is a geometric plane and the surface of the earth is an approximate sphere); and partly from his uncritical conflation of sites of very different dates. In your case however, the proposed route is very far from being a straight line, either on the map or on the ground; and the natural indicators that you suggest are exactly the same kind that any traveller in wild and mountain country will use, today and in the remote past.

I don't think that I can usefully say more than this, simply because in the last resort, as I have indicated above, the acceptance or rejection of an hypothesis of this kind can rest only on personal preference.

Yours sincerely

R. J. C. Atkinson

[Professor Atkinson was kind enough to read the MS just before publication and to give us permission to print his letter. Ed]

Reading List

[We attach Alan Shore's reading list, obviously because you may wish to learn more about Wales, prehistoric travel, Celtic history, the Celtic church and Old Straight Tracks. Not all the books have a lot to say on his theme, for example, we are not aware that George Borrow has much to contribute. However the list brings home Alan's enthusiasm and pleasure in delving around in pursuit of his grand idea. Ed]

Anglo Saxon England   Ed. Peter Amoes 1972
Along the Roman Roads of Britain   J H B Peel
Along the Green Roads of Britain   J H B Peel
The Green Roads of England   R Hippsley Cox 1914

Britain in the Dark Ages   Ordnance Survey
Britain and Ireland in Early Christian Times 1971
Britain in the Roman Empire   Joan Liversidge 1968
Britain, Rome's Most Northerly Province   G M Durrend 1969
Britain and the Western Seaways   E G Bowen 1972
Brut y Twysogion. (Chronicle of the Princes)   Thomas Jones

Celtic Britain   Nora Chadwick 1968
Celt & Saxon - studies in the Early English Border
                  Ed. Nora K Chadwick 1972
The Celtic Realms   Dillon & Nora Chadwick
The Celts - Ancient People and Places   T G E Powell 1958
Christianity in Britain - 300 to 700 AD Eds. Barley & Hanson 1978
Companion Guide to North Wales Elizabeth Beasley & Peter Howell 1975
Companion Guide to South Wales 1977

Dark Age Britain   Henry March 1970
Digging up our Past   Ifor Edwards 1955
The Drovers Roads of Wales   Fay Godwin & Shirley Toulson 1977

Early British Trackways, Moats, Mounds, Camps and Sites
                  Alfred Watkins 1922
The Early Christian Monuments of Wales   V Nash Williams 1950
Everyday Life in Roman and Anglo Saxon Times   1959
Exploring Wales   William Condry 1970

Sir Gawain and the Green Knight   Tolkein 1975
Giraldus Cambrensis. The Itinerary through Wales Trans. R C Hoare
A Guide to the Prehistoric Monuments of England & Wales
                  Jaquetta Hawkes

An Historical Atlas of Wales   William Rees
A History of Wales   Sir John Lloyd
The History of the Isle of Man   R H Kinvig 1950
Home Travels - A Tour of Wales   Thomas Pennant 1775

Isle of Man and Atlantic Britain   R H Kinvig 1958
An Introduction to the History of Wales   A H Williams 1962

King Arthur   Norma Lorre Goodriche 1986

The Ley Hunters Manual   Alfred Watkins 1927
Ley Lines in Question   T Williamson & Liz Bellamy 1983

The Matter of Wales   Jan Morris 1984
The Mabinogion, trans.   Lady Charlotte Guest 1877

The Old Straight Track   Alfred Watkins 1925

Packway to Motorway, North West   John Compton 1974
Personality of Britain (ancient routeways)   Sir Cyril Fox 1943
Prehistoric Britain   Keith Branigan 1976
Prehistoric and Early Wales Foster and Daniel 1965
Pre Roman Britain   Stanley Thomas 1965

The Quest for Merlin   Nickolai Tolstoy 1985

Regional Archaeologies - North Wales   Kathleen Watson 1965
Roads. Past into Present Series   Hugh Bodley 1971
Roads and Tracks of Britain   Christopher Taylor 1979
Roman Britain   John Walker 1978
Roman Britain, Outpost of Empire   Scullard 1979
Roman Land Surveyors   C A W Dilke 1971
The Roman Frontier in Wales   V Nash Williams 1969
Roman Roads in Britain   Ivan Margary 1967
Roman Roads of Europe   N H H Sitwell 1981

In Search of the Dark Ages   Michael Wood 1981
Stage Coaches in Wales   Herbert Williams 1977
The Settlement of the Celtic Saints in Wales   E G Bowen 1956

Visions of the Past   Christopher Taylor and Richard Muir 1983

Wales: an Archaeological Guide   Chris Houlder 1974
Wales Through the Dark Ages Vol 1   Ed. A. Roterick 1959
Who Are The Welsh   Glyn Daniel 1954